COURSE

PRICING

STRATEGIES

*Your Guide to Confidently
Pricing Your Online Course*

LUCAS MARINO

AUTHOR, *MONETIZE YOUR BOOK WITH A COURSE*

COURSE PRICING STRATEGIES

*Your Guide to Confidently
Pricing Your Online Course*

LUCAS MARINO
AUTHOR, *MONETIZE YOUR BOOK WITH A COURSE*

TABLE OF CONTENTS

INTRODUCTION

Welcome, creators!

The last time we connected was through my book *Monetize Your Book with a Course.*

If you built that course, congratulations!

Monetize Your Book with a Course contained many great topics related to course building. However, some topics were simply too big to fit into that book without detracting from its primary mission of helping you create a profitable course from your book.

Pricing your course is one of those big topics. To some, this is the biggest challenge of hosting a course.

No worries, friend. In this book, I will guide you through *course pricing strategies.* I will share the dos and don'ts with you so that you can make informed decisions on pricing your products.

I'll share how to price your course logically while always prioritizing your learners' interests.

Then, I will address some of the other questions you probably have:

- Should I check my competitors' prices?
- When pricing my course, how important is it to consider the valuable outcome for my learners? (Okay, you know this one, but it's critically important for us to discuss.)
- How do I accurately cover my costs in my pricing strategy?
- Should I offer sales discounts and run promotions to boost sluggish sales?
- When is it appropriate to raise and lower my course prices?
- What does the volume and price relationship even mean?
- Do I really need to collect sales taxes?
- How do I approach bundling products like courses, communities, live events, and books?

These are very smart questions to ask!

Let's get down to the business of pricing your course so it benefits your bottom line.

Are you ready?

CHAPTER ONE

WHY IS PRICING
SO DIFFICULT?

Pricing courses is, without a doubt, the most subjective topic I'm asked about when helping clients create courses. Pricing feels so personal. We attach the value of our hard work, time, emotional investment, expectations, and potential to the price of products that we've created.

This is a very healthy perspective or situation, but it's also a slippery slope. The value of your course is about much more than what you initially think. In the end, it's not how you feel about your product that matters most.

> WHAT MATTERS MOST IS THE BUYER'S
> PERCEIVED VALUE OF YOUR COURSE.

In simpler terms, it's what your customer thinks your course is worth. Note that this is not the same as the time or money you invested in developing the course.

Your customer may not understand how much you spent to put your course together. They have no clue whether it is your life's work. They don't care whether you spent days, weeks, months, or years assembling it. So, your marketing, societal and industry norms, and expectations inform their perceived value.

How many dollars does their problem cost them? What impact does their problem have on them?

People often assume that the solution to a problem will cost as much as the problem does or a little more.

That's normally how prices work. So, when considering the customer's or learner's perception of value, there are a few things you can influence (control) and a few things you cannot.

You cannot influence their expectations based on the following:

- their upbringing
- their prior experiences
- their personality
- their behaviors
- their experience with value

You also can't control your competitors' prices, the message sent by competitive marketing, or in most cases, the cause of their problem.

These things are out of your control. The influence of those elements on their perception of value isn't worth spending too much time on because you can't control the uncontrollables. However, you most *definitely* can control the controllables.

So, what are the controllables? Well, they include the following:

- your marketing **effort** (I refer to this as your Give-a-Damn factor)
- how you talk about the **value** your course provides to learners
- how you define, develop, deliver, and **market** your solution
- the **price** you place on your course
- **where** you market your course
- the **quality** of your **landing or sales page**
- and, the realistic **value of the solution** to their problem

In the following chapters, we'll unpack the four main variables you may consider when pricing your courses.

I caution those seeking a prebaked answer. There isn't a cut-and-dried, tried-and-true, never-fails equation.

There is no chart of course prices that dictates industry standards.

In fact, there is no standard, and my earlier statement about pricing being very subjective is about the surest thing in the entire topic of pricing. It is and always will be subjective.

But we can be very *selective* with how we approach our pricing. We can use prices for much more than just figuring out how much to collect for a course.

Pricing is powerful. This is one reason we feel pressured to get it right. Our pricing can make our course more or less accessible, set us apart from competitors, present a top-shelf image, and screen our clients.

Don't worry. After you read this book, you'll feel much more confident about developing a price structure that works for your courses and business.

CHAPTER TWO

FOUR POINTS FOR BUILDING YOUR COURSE PRICING STRATEGY

When pricing courses, I consider a minimum of four key considerations.

1. Competitor prices

2. The value of the outcome for the learner

3. The cost of course delivery and format

4. Industry norms and learner spending habits

Why is this important? Context matters! Thinking about these four points can help you comprehend your learners' buying and learning experiences. These four points influence their perception of cost. As I outlined in the opening chapter, their perception is very important.

You want to *see* the landscape of the industry as your buyers do. Your course will go to battle on the terrain of that landscape. If you win the battle, you win the sale. If you lose the battle, you lose the sale.

Let's dig in.

COMPETITOR PRICES

A message from the Land of the Obvious: course creators should research competitor prices.

This is common sense, right? Knowing competitor prices is a good thing. But we must not fall into the trap of blindly adopting competitor prices as our own.

Why not? What's the point of knowing our competitors' prices if we will not adopt them?

> **BEING FAMILIAR WITH YOUR COMPETITORS' PRICES HELPS YOU UNDERSTAND THE PLAYING FIELD.**

I encourage you to create a list of your competitors. Then, find the course or program that most resembles yours and see how they structure their offer. Check out how they talk about the value of their course.

Capture the pros and cons of their site. What are they doing well? What are they doing poorly?

Is their website attractive? Do they speak directly and clearly to the buyer? Do they list course features?

Write it down. Keep going.

Here is a sample list of things to capture:

- Is the website attractive?
- What price is listed?
- *Is* the price listed?
- Is there a good problem statement?
- Is there a clearly proposed solution?
- Is the course format explained?
- Is the course length advertised?
- Is there a live course component?
- Is there downloadable content?
- Is access to a community provided?
- Are discounts on other products available to enrolled learners?
- Is there an expiration on course access, or is lifetime access provided?
- Is there a one-on-one interaction between the learner and the instructor? Or is it self-paced? Or group coaching?

Now that you have this list of features for your competitor's course, you can see that the value is based on much more than just a price. The price should reflect the value of those features.

How would you feel if you were in the market searching for this course and you saw that price?

Now use that lens to look at your course.

I'm encouraging you to compare more than prices. I'm encouraging you to compare *all the value points.*

> **YOUR COURSES AND HOW YOU PRESENT THEM TO POTENTIAL BUYERS MAY DIFFER FROM YOUR COMPETITORS.**

This is one reason you shouldn't blindly adopt a competitor's price.

Another reason is what I call the *pricing death spiral.* If you and a competitor are looking at each other, and you both decide to compete on price, you'll race each other to the bottom of the market. As one of you lowers your prices to beat the competition, the other will respond by lowering their price accordingly.

This cycle may repeat until both of you have lowered your prices to the point of barely making any money.

All the while, your customers, and maybe your competitor, are unaware that this is your pricing strategy.

If one of you doesn't become responsible and stop the madness, you'll price yourselves right to the bottom of the market. You'll be in a high-volume, low-price world of misery. Eventually, other competitors will step into the market, out-compete you on quality, and win at a higher price point.

The market will perceive you as a low-price, low-value solution, and not everyone wants the low-price, low-value solution. More on this later.

That's enough negativity for one day. Let's get back to the positives, shall we?

You've researched your competitors and listed their prices and all their features. You understand the lay of the land a bit more now. Maybe you are now the proud owner of a spreadsheet that lists every competitor's name and all the features of their courses, including prices. You can see the industry trends for price and features. What now?

It's time to decide where you want to stand in the competition. Do you want to be on the higher end of the price scale? Or do you want to be in the middle or lower ranges of the scale? Maybe you want an offer in each area of the scale via multiple courses.

Perhaps you plan to start in the lower or middle price ranges and slowly move up as your course becomes more popular.

Regardless of your strategy, be intentional about where you position yourself in the market. Ask yourself, is this the identity of my business? Is this who I am, and does my product reflect that?

Let's wrap this thing up!

1. You researched your customers and captured all the features and prices of your competitors.

2. Now you analyze your business and your course's features and functions.

Position yourself on that same piece of paper with your competitors. Be as unbiased as you can, which is hard to do. Be honest with yourself.

Where do you fall on price?

Where do you fall on features?

Where do you fall on value compared to the rest of the group?

List your course in the group you want to be in, then adjust your profile accordingly. If you need to raise your price a bit, raise it. If you need to raise the quality of your product's landing page, raise it. Do what you must do to become what you want to be. Be intentional about what your business and your courses are.

This is how you use the price and position of your competitors to influence your own price and position. Be better because of this!

THE VALUE OF THE OUTCOME FOR THE LEARNER

Remember, learners don't buy courses; *they buy outcomes.* They really want what the course can help them achieve: a new outcome.

They show up with a problem to solve. Your course provides a solution, and there is an outcome associated with this!

When the learner solves their problem with your solution, what outcome will they achieve?

As I state in my book *Monetize Your Book with a Course,* the outcomes of a course may be generic or very specific, but they must always be valuable to the learner.

Upon completion of your course, a learner may do something that brings them value.

Knowing the value of that outcome is very important for your pricing.

A great example of this in modern business is the prevalence of professional certification training. People pay good money to gain *relevant* professional certifications because they usually lead to more income. Or maybe the person has a better chance of getting a competitive job because employers highly desire their certification. Hello, competitive edge!

In these cases, the outcome has *actual value* for the learner. They will pay for that opportunity because it brings them *more* opportunities.

If your course leads to a valuable outcome, consider a higher enrollment fee than courses that cannot offer the same value.

The price should be higher when demand is higher and the outcome is specific and valuable.

If your course does not lead to a specific and valuable outcome for the learner, you may have a hard time charging a substantial price.

Value increases demand.

There is a high demand for training in lucrative fields.

Demand is high when incomes are affected.

Demand is high when your course saves people significant time, opens doors, or improves opportunities for people.

If your course does none of these things, consider whether sufficient demand exists for your course to be priced in the upper half of its industry.

For example, if two course providers offer project management training, but only one provides the mandatory training required to sit for a certification exam...well, put yourself in the buyer's shoes. Which would you pay for?

This brings me to the point about the need for buyers to understand the relationship between what you teach and their desired outcome. If they can't easily see that your course gets them to that outcome, you need to consider what you are truly selling them.

Your competition is different if your course is primarily informative and doesn't bring the learner closer to a valuable outcome. You are now competing with every free YouTube video, moderately priced book, and informative blog about your topic.

Okay, I'm usually way more optimistic and upbeat than this. Let's end on a positive note, shall we?

I firmly believe there is a student for every course, and someone out there wants your course!

Valuable outcomes simply increase the probability that there will be more of those people willing to pay a premium for the course. Sell valuable courses, and your learners will better respond to your marketing and prices.

THE COST OF COURSE DELIVERY

When we create a course, we create an obligation. We must deliver and maintain that course so it can serve our business and others. When you price courses, think about the cost of properly delivering on that obligation.

What *must* you do to sustain and deliver the course in the chosen format?

I can hear you saying now, *Wait a minute, dude, didn't you tell me not to price according to time and materials?* Yes, I did (thank you for paying attention). And I promise you I'm not contradicting that advice.

In on-demand or self-paced courses, we don't base the price on the price of doing business plus a profit.

The more you move toward live or interactive hybrid environments, the more you should consider the time and materials involved.

Why?

In an on-demand course, you can sell the course passively and deliver it with little or no interaction with your students. This eliminates the delivery time and materials. That's the big distinction. We're talking about delivery and maintenance, not development. In my opinion, the development of online courses is a sunk cost.

I'm sure there will be some cost purists who will argue with me about this. That's cool. But, if I'm buying your self-paced, on-demand course, I'm not trading time for money with you in the direct fashion that live courses have in their DNA: live interaction between the learner and the instructor.

In self-paced online courses, we normally spread the cost of doing business across the sale of many courses. You can take the cost of your learning management system (LMS), your customer relationship management software (CRM), and all the things you use to run and deliver your course, figure out your break-even point, and make that a minimum target for sales.

This will help you break even on your investment. After you reach the break-even point, every dollar is profit.

For this reason, I calculate the cost of delivering my courses every year. Here are some common cost sources for my online courses:

- Thinkific learning management system (LMS)
- Keap Pro customer relationship management software (CRM)
- QuickBooks (business accounting)
- Google Workspace (email host)
- DropInBlog accounts (blogging)
- Wobo accounts (digital workbooks)
- Advertising

Sum the cost of these items for the year. Then, divide that by twelve. This is the average monthly overhead cost for your platform, not just this one course. If you only have one course, the full burden is on that course. But if you have multiple courses, you spread the overhead cost across multiple offers.

HYBRID COURSES

How is this any different in a hybrid environment? Hybrid courses contain both self-paced learning and live components. The live component is where the most significant cost lives.

Why? Because you have an opportunity cost. If you weren't on that live call, you could make your hourly coaching or consulting rate working with a client.

If you're teaching live or hosting a live question-and-answer (Q&A) session for the course, then you're giving up the opportunity to make money doing something else. You're injecting more of your personal time into the offer, and that can justifiably affect your price.

So, what is that impact? Well, you can bake your hourly rate into those sessions. But you'll probably overprice your offer depending on how many live Q&A sessions you offer, the topic, and all the things that go into pricing that we've discussed.

This is not as clean as simply saying, "Okay, I presented for one hour, and I should just add an hour to my rate." You can do that, but you'll need a substantial commitment from your learners to pay that much money.

If your hourly rate is what it should be, it's one of the most expensive rates in your business. For example, if your hourly rate is $250 an hour for coaching and consulting, that's the opportunity cost of hosting a live group Q&A session or teaching live. You're obligating an hour of coaching or consulting at the highest rate in your portfolio. You shouldn't price every live Q&A session at $250 because multiple people attend, each with a unique context that can't be fully addressed in a group session with others. The time is shared. Also, if you offer multiple live Q&A sessions, the price could quickly become too high.

LIVE COURSES

The next form of course delivery is a fully live course with on-demand content as reference or support materials. Here, you teach your course live, whether in person face-to-face or over a digital platform like Zoom, Teams, live streaming, or some other digital means.

Here, you're investing your personal time to deliver each course. You commit hours of teaching and discussion. This has an opportunity cost. Again, you can justify the cost or value of your time in the course price.

You adopt a substantial opportunity cost when you teach live for extended periods. For example, you may deliver thirty-two hours of instruction to a live on-site audience over four days. You charge $2,000 per student for that on-site session. You may deliver the live virtual version of that course for a different price (normally equal to or less than the on-site course).

The reason for the price difference is simple: convenience and cost. In the live virtual format, you don't have to pay for travel, reserved facilities, lodging, and rented technology (e.g., on-site Wi-Fi, projector or smart TV, printed materials). It has nothing to do with the curriculum.

There is a convenience for the students as well. They can attend training from the comfort of their homes, offices, or...wherever! They can also access the recordings after you deliver the live sessions. The learner can easily view recorded lessons if they miss some class time because of an emergency. In short, flexibility and convenience have value.

For in-person courses, I recommend setting a minimum number of enrolled students before traveling. For example, for my $2,000 in-person courses, I require a minimum of eight students. If you want me to travel for a course, it will be a $16,000 investment or more.

Since I mentioned travel, let's address how to price it. I recommend charging travel costs *separately from* the cost of course delivery. Provide your client with estimated travel costs based on current prices for plane tickets, rental cars, parking, gas, and everything you need. Pad the estimate by 10 percent to protect against market fluctuation.

You can quote the price of student enrollment and charge them for actual travel costs once your trip is complete. Don't forget to keep your receipts!

INDUSTRY NORMS AND BUYER HABITS

Habits are powerful, and norms are powerful. Put them together, and you know where you stand.

The behaviors that we create for ourselves guide us through many of our actions each day. Some people have a habit of staying up late. Others develop a habit of going to bed early. The next morning, each reaps what they've sowed.

Buyer habits are equally influential. And they are baked into us from a very young age.

The people and powerhouses in industries create an environment for pricing and purchasing goods. For example, think about the book market. When you walk into a bookstore or log onto an online book retailer, you expect to see particular book characteristics and pay a certain amount for a specific type of book in a particular genre. Am I right?

You may expect to pay between $25 and $50 for a popular hardback fiction book. You may expect to pay between $10 and $20 for the same book in paperback.

I love using book examples because books have been around for a long time. Books have been accessible to the public since the invention of the printing press. Over time, the price came down enough to get books in the hands of the commoners. Yes, that's you and me.

We've been buying books for a while, with the industry mostly controlled by those who owned presses and distribution channels. They set prices after they refined production costs and determined what people would pay.

Over time, the industry has established norms and buyer expectations. Indie publishing is shaking things up, but the results aren't causing monumental price shifts, are they?

I mentioned genres because you'll likely pay much more for a textbook than a typical best-selling hardcover fiction book.

We know the textbook industry drives high prices. Everyone and their mom in that market is trying to cash in on the "requirement" to have a specific textbook for a course. Authors, publishers, schools, and everyone in between profit from textbook sales. And, of course, they charge more for it because…it's a textbook. When I was in college, I used to be frustrated with textbook prices and always bought them used. I had little money. I was paying for things as I went, and textbooks were a hefty price. And I was almost never let down.

What about buyer expectations? When I buy a book, I part with some cash to get it. But truly, my real investment is time. The time I spend reading and the experience of that time are what I'm really buying.

I expect my experience with a book to be equal to or more than the cost. Or at least I perceive it to be, and I understand that price to be appropriate. I've created an expectation in my mind of what I'm willing to pay for a book based on my experience with past books and the norms established by the industry.

Now, if you priced that same hardcover fiction book discussed earlier like a textbook, I'd fall out of my chair in shock! (Yes, I'm that dramatic about books.)

A fiction book for $250? No thanks. I think I'll wait until it comes out as an eBook.

Some people will laugh at that and say, "Yeah, that's absurd. I would never pay $250 for a piece of fiction." And why is that?

Why are we willing to pay more for a textbook than the latest fiction novel? Even better, why are we willing to pay so much more for a textbook than we are for a nonfiction book that can turn a business or life around?

Books in the higher education industry are seen as being of greater value than regular nonfiction books. Your college courses cost a lot of money, and courses at a university cost more than those at a community college.

And you expect that!

There are many reasons for this, and I will not get into them here. Whether or not you think it's worth it, people often pay what the industry establishes as a normal price. There's been a point of balance between the industry and the buyer established over *years* of behavior.

The companies and governing bodies know they've conditioned consumers. Changing that conditioning takes time and deliberate action.

This sounds like both good and bad news, right? Good because there appear to be fewer restrictions, and bad because there seems to be less guidance.

The online course industry is a baby compared to the music, television, movie, and book industries. These industries have been around much longer than online commerce and the public internet.

We will form expectations in the coming years. For now, no single entity or industry is telling online educators how to price products.

It simply is not happening, and I think that's a good thing. There are no handcuffs! There are no restrictions! The decision for price starts with you, the course creator, and ends with the buyer. You set a price, and if the buyer feels it is fair, they exchange their money for your course. In the ideal case, this is mutually beneficial.

Great, Lucas. What am I supposed to do with this Wild West environment? How do I use this?

> **I CANNOT OVERSTATE THE IMPORTANCE OF THE "KNOW, LIKE, AND TRUST" FACTOR IN THE WORLD OF ONLINE COURSES.**

There are two people involved in that equation: *you and your buyers!*

Look at how much your buyers typically spend on a course like yours. What industry does your course exist in? Who are your competitors? Consider the questions we've been asking in this book.

Then, dive into the *you* part. That's always the most fun.

How you present your business significantly affects the expectations of potential buyers (your potential learners).

Which of these two entrepreneurs do you expect to charge higher course rates?

Option 1 – An experienced consultant who regularly charges $250 an hour for one-on-one sessions (and gets it) and hosts their course on a professional LMS. They have a thriving social media presence, give out tons of valuable free content, offer live Q&A sessions, and have a laundry list of testimonials on their site.

Option 2 – A consultant who regularly charges $50 an hour for one-on-one sessions (and gets it) and hosts their course on a low-price e-commerce platform. They have little social media presence, have no live components in the course, only list two products on their website, and don't share testimonials.

Which presents a higher perceived value based on your expectations as a buyer?

Which would you *expect* to charge more for their course?

Now the magic question: If you had the money, which would you pay $1,000 to learn from?

You have the freedom to define what you will charge based on your reputation, the cost of your products, and the value you build into your offers. More value = more pricing freedom.

Whether you sell high- or low-priced courses, your buyers expect you to follow the golden rule and always provide more value than the sticker price.

> **THE VALUE OF YOUR COURSE SHOULD *ALWAYS* EXCEED THE STICKER PRICE.**

Once you've decided on that sticker price, you can decide how you'd like to collect the money. Do you want to collect a one-time fee, offer payment plans, or set up a subscription? Chapter Three will help you decide which options are best for you and your buyers.

SINGLE PAYMENTS, PAYMENT PLANS, AND SUBSCRIPTIONS

When we think of course prices, we often think of one price. However, course prices can exist in many configurations. Each approach has its own pros and cons, and this chapter will help you decide which price options are best for your courses.

ONE-TIME PURCHASE

One-time purchase is the most common approach. You charge a single price and receive a single payment. That's it!

If the course costs $500, the buyer pays that $500 to enter the course, and the deal is done.

The one-time payment option is the simplest and most common option for pricing most products and services.

PAYMENT PLANS

Payment plans allow your purchaser to pay you over several payments. If you charge $500 for the course but offer a five-month payment plan, the purchaser will pay you every month for five months until they've fully paid the balance.

Usually, the monthly rate is fixed, not variable. The purchaser makes the first payment and gains access to the course. Then, they pay a set amount each month for the term.

I recommend you charge an additional fee for this luxury. It benefits you to receive full payment at purchase. Payment plans benefit your customer, and that should come with a small fee.

For example, you charge $500 for a course. The purchaser opts into your five-month payment plan. Rather than have them pay you five payments of $100, you could require five payments of $120. You've given them the convenience of monthly payments and recouped a 20 percent fee for the inconvenience (or risk) of not receiving full payment at the start.

Another payment plan option is to front-load the first payment. In this approach, you can sell the $500 course but offer a payment plan that includes an initial cost of $200 with four follow-on payments of $100.

So, what's the difference between a payment plan and a subscription?

COURSE SUBSCRIPTION

A course subscription allows the purchaser to pay a set fee each month to access your course. If the purchaser stops their subscription, they lose access to the course material. This should be very familiar. Subscription models surround us! All your television and music streaming platforms are subscription based.

There are two barriers to hosting via subscription. The first is that course hosts worry the students will gobble up all the course material and cancel their subscriptions. Well, that may happen. But I challenge you to think big and offer them so much value that they don't want to leave! Improve the subscription value by dripping new lessons weekly or monthly, giving access to an online community, or hosting exclusive events for subscribers.

The second concern is tracking and charging the monthly subscriptions! Well, friends, you can probably predict my solution at this point. Use a professional LMS to automate that for you! Thinkific Payments processes my monthly subscriptions and payments. I review and reconcile issues each week. It's part of the game when you offer subscriptions and payment plans.

One note of caution on subscription pricing—don't undercharge for a course. Obviously, a $1,000 course shouldn't also be available for a $20 monthly subscription fee. Do the math; the learner would have to pay for fifty months for you to meet the usual sticker price of the course. That's bonkers. Don't be bonkers.

So, what the heck is the difference between a subscription and a site membership?

SITE MEMBERSHIP

A site membership provides access to all content on a site, not just a single course or community. That's right; you can charge one monthly membership fee to access *everything* on your site!

For one membership fee, the member can access every product you allow. You could offer one fee for access to all courses, communities, products, and events on your site. This is a great option if you stack content with a smile. In the membership model, you aren't concerned with the individual value of your products; you provide a world of value for a monthly fee.

The membership model works great when you have many products and a diverse offer. I have worked with course providers who host a catalog of courses, all aimed at educating and entertaining a particular audience. They use an online community to address course topics, lessons, articles, common interests, and events. Again, the membership needs sufficient content to keep people engaged and coming back for more. Your job as a membership host is to keep engaging and valuable content flowing consistently!

COMBINING PRICE OPTIONS

You can offer multiple price options if you want to improve the accessibility of your course. This is a common practice for course hosts who serve clients in a variety of income brackets.

For example, you may offer a $3,000 course. That won't be an issue for some buyers and will be slightly out of reach for others. If both buyers are in your ideal client pool, offering a payment plan may help the more price-conscious buyers. You could offer a one-time purchase price of $3,000 and a payment plan that includes an initial payment of $1,500 with two follow-on monthly payments of $1,000. Then, let the buyers decide which investment is best for them.

Spend some time thinking about how much of a fee you want to charge for the payment option. You may opt to avoid additional fees, but I encourage you to reconsider so you can make the additional burden worth your while.

You could provide a third subscription option if you wanted. You could charge $250 a month, and it would take a full year of subscription to break even on the offer. Does that sound reasonable based on the normal engagement time a paying customer spends with your course or community? If not, change the rate. Aim for a realistic period. It doesn't make sense to charge a rate that takes twelve months to reach the regular price if the course normally engages clients for three months. Make sense?

Let's finish our conversation about pricing options and look at time and materials pricing. You've been around this practice your whole life. It's the best way to price products, right? Not quite.

CHAPTER FOUR

AVOID PRICING BY TIME AND MATERIALS

Pricing an online course according to your investment of time and materials is a surefire way to price yourself right out of a profit.

Your course is a digital product that more than one user will consume. This is one reason pricing a course by time and materials is a poor practice.

Let's unpack this a bit. What does this mean?

Well, when you price something by time and materials, you literally count every hour and resource you used to create and deliver your course. You count the hours you recorded audio or video, wrote the text, assembled the course materials, built the LMS pages and settings, and the list goes on.

You also count some of the cost of cameras and microphones, recording software, office space, and energy consumed. You could get down to the nitty-gritty when calculating time and materials.

Count the number of hours that you invested and multiply that by your hourly rate for production and delivery. Does that number look right to you? Not likely. That's never going to work with a digital product.

As a consumer, I appreciate your invested time and money to develop a quality course by using quality materials and methods. But I'm not willing to repay you dollar for dollar for that investment *by myself.*

An online course priced by time and materials would seem astronomically priced. It doesn't make sense to the purchaser.

Let's go through a quick example.

Simply recording a course with good equipment in your home office would be costly for your student. You would most likely price your course out of competition or well above what your learner will pay for a course of this magnitude.

That was the best-case scenario; let's look at the other end of the scale.

In this example, you used higher-quality equipment and invested in videography services and animations. You created multiple downloads or even an entire workbook and then used advanced software to facilitate the course elements.

You also invested several hours at the higher end of the scale for labor. In the end, you could have invested $35,000 in the course. Because of how time and material pricing works, could you then turn around and charge each student $35,000 for that online course?

You get the point.

Although you should always know your investment in developing a product, this method does not prove logical for pricing your course.

Some of you are saying, *Those examples don't reflect my situation. I deliver live courses or hybrid courses.* Well, that justifies increasing the price because live components typically add value.

That's not a license to use a one-to-one ratio across the board. You could deliver the same live course virtually and charge more because of the interaction and exclusivity factor.

The learner gets group or one-on-one time with you, asks detailed specific questions, and receives answers in real time.

And usually, content added to the online course material adds value. That added value allows you to increase the price of the course or offer a live element, and that live element adds additional cost to the base course.

Let's use an example of $1,000 for an online course. You then charge an additional $1,000 for the live sessions, once a month, for the lifetime of the course.

You can see how the waters get muddied with course pricing.

It would be wonderful if time and materials pricing were effective for pricing online courses. We'd simply keep track of everything we were doing and spending, tally it up, and have our magic price.

It would be easy to calculate but would be very expensive for learners. It is inevitable for you to spend time and materials developing your course.

> **THEN YOU SPREAD THAT COST OVER YOUR ENTIRE LEARNER BASE.**

So, what do you do?

You need to consider how many students it would take to break even on your course. What's your break-even point on your investment?

Let's say you invest eight hours in developing course materials. Your typical hourly coaching rate is $200 an hour, so you're sitting on $1,600 worth of labor. Then you spend another eight hours loading the course into the course platform and building the landing page. You've spent another $1,600, so you have $3,200 in labor on the books.

Now let's look at the cost of your software. Your LMS costs you $100 a month, and you paid $40 for software to create your PDFs. Your camera was $180, and your microphone was $180. Added up, we're looking at a total beginning cost of $3700 in labor and software. Now calculate the number of students needed to break even at your desired course price.

This is a relatively low-cost investment for online courses. In fact, you can easily spend ten times this amount developing a course. If you sold this course for $500, you would break even at eight students. That is a very fair expectation. I'm not thinking twice about that; I'm rolling with it.

As you can see, pricing by time and materials doesn't work very well for courses. Remember that the purchaser will pay a price equal to or less than the value of the outcome. Time and material costs normally far exceed that value for a single purchase. There are always exceptions to every scenario, but generally, this is how it goes.

At this point, you should have a healthy understanding of how to think about your pricing strategy. Now, let's shift our focus to how the valuable relationship with affiliates and revenue share partners may affect your price.

CHAPTER FIVE

AFFILIATE AND REVENUE SHARES

Affiliates and revenue share partners play an important role in your pricing strategy.

If you have affiliates or revenue share partners and you've never considered their impact on pricing before, this may surprise you.

But what the heck are these two things?

I covered this topic extensively in my book *Monetize Your Book with a Course*. The following modified conversation is from that book for the benefit of those who have not read it. If you have already read it, I promise that rereading the information will not harm you. (I embedded no subliminal messages in the content.)

Affiliates are people who advertise your products, and in return, you reimburse them with a percentage of each sale or a set amount of each sale.

For example, if I were an affiliate for your course, you would provide me with a link to sell your course. When someone used my link to buy your course, I would automatically earn a percentage of that sale or a set fee. We motivate affiliates to promote your products for profit.

Normally, you choose someone you want to advertise your product, and who will share your links with their network of clients, friends, family, and partners.

And you pay that person to do so when it results in a sale.

How is this different from a revenue partner?

Well, a revenue share partner earns a set amount of revenue from every sale of that product, no matter where it comes from. They don't have to be the seller or affiliate or have any relationship with the sale. Consider this as being a partner on a product.

When anyone buys your course for any reason, from any location or source, you entitle your revenue share partner to a certain share of that sale.

Normally, this is a fixed percentage.

It might be a fifty-fifty split if you teamed up with somebody to create the course, and you've agreed to split all revenue of the course equally. Sometimes this is a business, host, or instructor relationship. Perhaps you're an instructor, and you're paying someone to publish your courses on their LMS. As the instructor, you earn a revenue share for every sale, and as the host, they earn a revenue share for hosting the course.

Let's discuss the mindset and perspective you should have when considering affiliates or revenue share partners and the impact of those partnerships on your pricing strategy.

My book coach, mentor, and cofounder of the Empire Builders Masterclass, Honorée Corder, has a great saying.

> ## "I'D RATHER HAVE 50 PERCENT OF A WATERMELON THAN 100 PERCENT OF A GRAPE."

You may be asking what the heck watermelons and grapes have to do with selling courses.

Fair question!

When you give someone the opportunity to market your course and receive an affiliate share, you spread your marketing net further than you're capable of doing alone.

You're accessing their community, their network, and their audience.

Because of that access, you will make sales that you would most likely not have made, and you may make anywhere from 50 percent to 80 percent on that course rather than 100 percent by creating that affiliate opportunity. So basically, you're paying a fee of whatever affiliate share percentage you have established.

You're paying that fee to make sales that you would not have made on your own.

You would rather make a smaller percentage on those sales than not have made those sales at all, right?

One of the cool parts about affiliates is their motivation to succeed. They don't get paid to try. They get paid to land sales.

An affiliate usually only gets paid when a sale is made.

That is the magic of affiliate marketing. This is much different from paying a marketing agency or a sales team an hourly rate or a set project fee to go out and secure sales with or without a guarantee of actually doing so.

You basically pay an agency to try. You're paying them for their effort, and you're paying them for their expertise. But they can't promise you results.

Let's look at an example.

You could pay an affiliate 20 percent of a $100 course.

And every time a course sells with their affiliate link, they make $20, and you make $80.

They make $20 for making that sale for you, and you make $80 on a sale you would not have made on your own.

Now they're motivated to repeat this because they've earned some profit, and they like profit, and they like your product. So, they're going to want to sell more of your course.

And then both of you make more money.

And in this case, you've made 80 percent of that watermelon, baby.

You might see that example and think, *Well, it's only $20, or only 20 percent.* All right.

That's not a big deal.

But maybe you've heard that some people pay their affiliates up to 50 percent.

Yes, that's true.

Like so many other pricing elements, there is no set standard for affiliate rates.

You can pay an affiliate as much as you feel comfortable paying them.

Just make sure you pay them enough to make it worth their while.

It must be realistic.

If you want to motivate people to market or sell your products for you, you need to reward them for doing so with an appropriate share of the revenue.

I'm a big fan of affiliate revenue.

I only promote products I've used or services I've hired. I sell nothing I don't have experience with.

I want you to understand that mindset. Your affiliates need to see your product before they'll be comfortable selling it as well. That means you will need to provide your affiliates with access to your materials. You could sell them your course at full price, sell them your course at a discounted price, or give them access to your course for free.

Again, there is no standard. It's all about what you and the affiliate are comfortable with.

Consider giving them access to that course either for free or for a minimum of the revenue share. Then provide them with a link as an affiliate and allow them to use that link to purchase your assets at a discount. They can then turn around and market and sell your course.

You can always do this by creating a discount coupon if you don't want to give them an affiliate link until they're done with the course. But you want to allow them to experience your course at a discount, whether with a partial discount or a fully free opportunity.

Can you see how an abundance mindset plays into this strategy? We let go of a scarcity mindset to make more money.

A scarcity mindset would say *don't let someone access this course to become an affiliate. Or, don't give someone that much affiliate share. I need to make every single dollar I can off this product.*

My question for you is why?

LET GO OF THAT SCARCITY MINDSET.

You willingly sacrifice the enrollment price for that person to attend your course. But the return on your investment could be many multiples of that cost.

I'm a big fan of this and do it openly and freely. If I know somebody long enough to gauge whether they'd be a good affiliate, I immediately offer it to them.

I don't just hand out my course for free to people, but I will give them a discount. And if there's someone close to me *I know, like, and trust*, I will provide them with free access.

They've invested in me by developing a relationship and forming trust with me. I reward that investment by providing them with free access to the course so that they can experience it. They can improve some aspects of their life, then turn around and become a champion for the course as an affiliate. Then they make money for both of us.

But if I've just recently met somebody and am not sure whether they would be the right marketing partner, I'll give them a discount.

If they don't want to sample the course, that's fine. I can still provide them with the affiliate opportunity.

You just need to be very careful about what people say about your product when they haven't experienced it. So, suppose you provide affiliate opportunities without requiring attendance to your course or program. In that case, giving them some preformatted sales copy is a good idea so they can speak intelligently about your product.

REVENUE SHARE PARTNERS

Let's switch and talk about revenue share partners because a revenue share partner differs from an affiliate.

A revenue share partner makes a share of the sale of a course no matter who sells it. They're basically like a creation partner, not just a marketing and sales partner.

They may have some significant role in creating your course, you cohost or co-own it, and that's why there's a revenue share.

You may host their course on your site, and they pay you a set fee for every enrollment in that course. That's a revenue share. That's different from affiliates; affiliates just market, and when a sale closes, they make some money on that success.

A revenue share partner, on the other hand, makes money on every course sale regardless of who makes the sale. They're a business partner.

So, what does this have to do with our pricing strategy? Well, if I have a revenue share partner with a fifty-fifty split, that means that every time someone enrolls in the course, that partner and I split the profits fifty-fifty.

I'm going to make a certain amount of money, they're going to make a certain amount of money, and we're both aware of that. And we know how much money we need to make as individuals to make this effort worth our while or at least worth exploring. So, we consider that in the price.

PRICING WITH AFFILIATE OR REVENUE SHARES

All right, so when I consider the price of the course, I must remember that my learner doesn't care whether I am paying affiliates to sell my course. They don't care whether I have a revenue share partner. It's not their thing to worry about. That is part of my business equation and my thinking strategy.

You shouldn't use revenue or affiliate shares as a reasonable justification for jacking up the price of your course; your learner would never sympathize with that because it doesn't provide them with any value. Remember, they're buying outcomes and value.

Your learners aren't going to pay $500 for a course when it's only worth $300 to them in value. You may think you have to charge $500 because of your overhead costs, and then you have affiliates and revenue share partners. But your learners will tell you to keep your course because that's not their problem.

If the course value is only $300, by measuring content and impact and by industry norms—all the things that matter to your learner—then that's what it's worth.

Maybe you're not in a good position to run this type of business. At least, that's what your learners are going to think.

They're not going to say anything, though. They just won't buy your product.

If your price is too high because of your costs, don't make it the learner's problem. The solution is not to factor that into the price. The solution is to sell more courses.

Take a moment to reflect on the volume and price relationship, then do the math to see what you could potentially earn as profit and determine whether the effort is good for you. (We will discuss more about the volume and price relationship in Chapter Eight.)

In a perfect world, you create everything. You market and sell everything just right, and everything works out great. And in the end, you make all the profit. But we usually benefit more when we have alliances, partners, and friends—people backing us up—working alongside each other for everyone's greater good.

And again, I work on both sides of this coin as an affiliate myself. I earn affiliate revenue, and I allow others to be an affiliate for me.

I also work on both sides of this situation for revenue shares. I have revenue share partners, and I am a revenue share partner to others.

The more, the merrier, my friends.

So, now your friends and business partners are along for the ride. They can promote your courses and spread your net to areas of the market you may not reach on your own. Wonderful!

Now, let's discuss how sales promotions fit into your pricing strategy.

CHAPTER SIX

RUNNING SALES PROMOTIONS

Running sales promotions or, in essence, offering special pricing to boost sales is a very effective and attractive proposition. Especially when sales seem hard to come by.

> I'M A BIG FAN OF OFFERING SPECIALS.
> BUT I'M ALSO A BIG FAN OF NOT
> RUNNING SPECIALS ALL THE TIME.

There are some dangers in discounting prices too often. We'll talk about that and other approaches to boosting sales in just a moment. First, let's discuss what sales promotions are and how they relate to regular prices.

Loosely speaking, a sales promotion is a special event that offers a discounted price (hopefully, still above sticker price) or some exceptional value.

Let's look at a few sales promotion examples.

In the first example, you sell something you own at a discount for a limited time.

Another approach is to bundle products together in a uniquely valuable way that saves the buyer money.

BOGO, anyone?

That's right. You, too, can buy one and get one free!

In this example, you didn't change the price tag. But you offered two products for the price of one.

You're probably saying, "Dude, I know, I get it. I see these things all the time. Why are you telling me this?"

Because we often forget there are ways to offer pretty sweet specials on our products without slashing our prices every five days.

Of course, I'm exaggerating with the five-day comment, but you know who you are.

When you go somewhere, and they are constantly running a sales promotion, it makes you wonder whether it's really a sale.

It also makes you wonder whether you should ever buy anything at the regular price.

Why not just wait? There's bound to be another sale on exactly what you're looking for within the next seventy-two hours because they're always launching sales.

Now we're back to talking about that buyer's psychology stuff.

Yes, you can give your buyers sales fatigue.

I am not motivated to buy a used car every day of the week. But I'll be damned if, in the 1980s and 90s, Big Al's wasn't running a sale every weekend.

In fact, that's what I associated Big Al with. Big Al's dealership was always running a sale, and you could always get a great sales price at Big Al's.

Is it just a great price, or is it a great sale? Is this really a special event?

Let's be honest here.

If you always offer the best price, then say that. You don't have to make it sound like it's on sale or being sold at a discount.

You can simply say, "Look, we just don't believe in overcharging for things, and we price them as low as we can every day."

People will appreciate that.

If you are going to run a sales promotion, consider an appreciable price drop and create urgency in other ways, like time. So, the first way to run a sale is to discount the price for a limited time.

The second way is to bundle products. Buy one, get one free. Buy one, get one half off is a combination of the two; you get it.

Another way is to sell at a very competitive price but only for a short period, and then the product comes off the market for a while.

Maybe now you're thinking a little differently about sales promotions. Although I haven't really told you anything you didn't already know.

> **WHAT WE'RE TRYING TO DO IS SELL A LARGER VOLUME OF PRODUCTS TO INDIVIDUALS IN A SINGLE PROMOTION OR EVENT.**

That's really what happens when we run sales promotions.

I hear you saying, "Now, Lucas, not every sale is a promotion, and not every sale is an urgent call for purchasers to scramble to the checkout before the deadline."

You are correct. Look at you. Aren't you smart!

I offer a loyal learner's discount on my site. If you've bought a course from me, you can apply a *loyal learner* discount coupon when enrolling in other courses on my website as a reward for your loyalty to my brand.

It is not a limited-time offer. I do not advertise or speak about it as a special event or promotion. It's always running. It's always there. And now I have to change the code because you know about it. I'm just kidding; you should definitely use it. (Yes, this is real. Go try it right now. The code is *loyallearner*. Then, use your new power for good in the world.)

But in all seriousness, the loyal learner's code exists on my site in some form 365 days a year, every year. I want people who purchase from me to know that I appreciate their willingness to buy from me again. Nothing more, nothing less.

I encourage you to reward your learners with some loyalty programs as well.

The promotion doesn't have to involve a discounted price. It could be exclusive access to a product you don't regularly sell or offer in any other way.

It tells them that once they're in, you'll provide them with these valuable things because they're loyal learners. And if they buy another class, I'd hook them up with more cool things!

But that promotion is only available to people who are repeat offenders in my business. You bought this book, so congrats! You are in the club.

If you read my book *Monetize Your Book with a Course,* you will recognize the following modified conversation. It bears repeating to benefit those who have not read the book because it's important that we talk more about sales fatigue.

> **I LIKE TO RUN SALES ON SPECIAL OCCASIONS AND ON SPECIAL OCCASIONS ONLY.**

For example, a course launch. It's your first public delivery, so why not offer a discount to get people interested?

Special occasions, company birthdays, and major events like summits and conventions are also great for running sales promotions.

Make the discount substantial enough to matter. You only save your client three dollars if the offer is a small 3 percent discount on a $100 course.

Offer a discount that's attractive enough, or you're basically wasting your time. It also might make you look a little funny when you brag about offering a 3 percent discount on a $100 course.

As in most things, there is a need for balance. You don't want to offer too small a discount, but you also do not want to give away the farm by offering too substantial a discount.

You might see people offer steep discounts when they get desperate for sales. They've invested all this time and money into building this product, but they're struggling with marketing and sales. They're not getting sales conversions on their site, and they get desperate.

So, they put a ridiculous discount on the course. Obviously, doing this could have a detrimental effect on how your network views your product's image. They wonder how good your product truly is if you offer such a deep discount.

There'd better be an exceptional circumstance explained clearly in your marketing copy. I would also avoid offering those big discounts annually; I mentioned before that you will condition your audience. Some people will literally wait to buy your product because they know you offer a discount every year. They'll just wait you out. Don't do that.

This approach also makes people question whether you're overcharging for your product regularly. I mean, if you can afford to give it away for a huge discount, why are you regularly charging so much for it?

Offering steep discounts can damage your product's price perception. Again, let's try to seek some balance.

So, now that we've discussed sales promotions, it's time to discuss when to consider raising or lowering your price.

CHAPTER SEVEN

WHEN TO RAISE OR LOWER YOUR PRICES

Let's talk about when to raise or lower your prices.

Project milestones, such as predevelopment launches, presales, or betas, may cause price changes. And other times, it's in response to customer demand.

A sale or change in the market creates a change in your business; one of those changes is in the product value.

All right, so let's talk about project milestones and project-related price changes first.

These events are typically associated with a new course release or a significant update. In rare instances, it may be a reduction in the price as you sunset the course.

Think of these milestones as part of the course life cycle. It starts early when you develop the course. Then you launch the course and maintain the course. Finally, you will eventually sunset or dispose of the course.

BETA LAUNCHING OR PRESELLING YOUR COURSE

In my book *Monetize Your Book with a Course,* I cover how to execute a predevelopment launch.

Essentially, you can test the market and see whether there's an interest in buying your course before you fully develop the curriculum. Once you see sufficient demand, you're obligated to produce the rest of the material. And off you go into Funtime course creation mode.

In these early presales or predevelopment launches, I like to offer the course to my beta learners at a significant discount. So, let's say I price a new course at $1,000. I will sell my beta for half of that ($500). The price goal for the future is $1,000. And I know I will deliver $1,000 worth of value, but I may not deliver it on day one. Or I may not convince people of that value on day one.

> I WILL USE PRICE AS LEVERAGE TO GET PEOPLE INTERESTED.

Then, over time, I'll work toward the target price of $1,000. The beta is a straightforward means of justifying that because it's early in the course development process.

Once the beta is done, I gather student feedback and testimonials about the course material. I'm exchanging 50 percent off my regular price for the learner's obligation to give me that feedback. This provides me with a solid foundation for a price increase.

I know I've increased the value once I've incorporated their suggested improvements into the course. I've tested the market, and I have a product that works. I now have the confidence to move my price closer to my target or even to go straight to my target price, depending on how the experience went.

These aren't laws, and there are no set rules or industry norms. These are just my recommendations and the behaviors I practice. This is the way I like to do business. And it also helps me sleep at night because I know I'm doing things in a fair way. I'm being reimbursed, and my learners are getting exceptional value.

It's okay if we find issues; I gave a discount for this purpose.

Once upon a time, I ran a beta, and I experienced some technical issues with the videos loaded on my LMS.

Because I had only charged my learners a beta price, they were patient while I resolved the tech issues. And I didn't feel absolutely terrible about it. We were working out the kinks together to make sure that everything was working right before we went live to the public.

Just being in that environment changes things because there will be some give and take.

LAUNCHING TO THE PUBLIC

After the beta, or the predevelopment launch, I raise the price. If I received and accepted feedback from the beta group that I should add value before increasing the price, then I do so before the public release.

If I get unanimous feedback from the beta group that the beta price at 50 percent was right, then I will do some hard thinking about whether I should increase my price.

I revisit the fundamentals. Perhaps I missed something. Or maybe I misread or misunderstood the impact of one of the *four pricing elements* I mentioned in Chapter Two.

As a reminder, there are four key considerations.

1. Competitor prices

2. The value of the outcome for the learner

3. The cost of course delivery and format

4. Industry norms and learner spending habits

> **AGAIN, THESE FOUR POINTS INFLUENCE THE LEARNER'S PERCEPTION OF COST.**

If I miss the mark on one of these, then I will make the adjustment and increase the price. After all, I added value and improved the product. It helped people, and they saw the value of the purchase.

If I did well on the predevelopment sale and the feedback, including pricing, was positive, I would go live with the full price.

I would have a major kickoff event like a webinar, workshop, or virtual summit. Create a buzz, get people talking, get people interested, and get people in the room. Educate people on the launch of the new course—maybe with a social media campaign.

We won't dive into course marketing here; this is a book on pricing. So, let's get back to the topic.

If I didn't have the confidence to go straight to my regular asking price after the beta, I would consider how to get there gradually. And I'd plan incremental increases over the next year.

Allow marketing and promotions to work and monitor purchaser behaviors.

We usually tap our warm market first. This means that most of the people in your close circle who will buy your course will buy it while it's in its beta or in its first release. They know the price is going to be lower. They're already interested in your product; they already know, like, and trust you. They're prime candidates for purchasing earlier rather than later.

Don't get flustered if sales slow after your course has been on the market. That's normal. It is not a powerful indicator that you've priced too high. Sales rarely provide enough data or insight to justify a price change.

It's not just about how many people sign up; it's about *who* signs up. It could be a couple of other factors. But the message here is don't point blank accept that the price is the cause just because it's the thing you're least confident about.

COURSE MAINTENANCE

Congratulations! Your course serves a stable flow of learners, and you've had a routine price increase. Your course is mature, like a fine wine. You've continuously added value where appropriate over the year. If this is the case, be confident in a price increase without losing sleep.

We live in interesting times, and I'd be remiss if I didn't mention world economics affecting pricing. But it's not the prime driver. Reconsider your price every year and increase it to cover inflation and increased hosting fees. An increase of 3 percent to 6 percent covers average inflation. In times of financial instability, consider holding your price.

Know exactly who your buyers are and how they are affected by the markets. Be sure they can afford an increase. People with less disposable income spend less on impulse buys.

You may notice a fluctuation in sales as the markets move. If you have a higher-priced course and cater to people with more expendable income, you may or may not see an appreciable change. These buyers and markets remain stable during market shifts. If you cater to buyers in lower income brackets, the market may affect you sooner.

Don't panic. Remember, you have control over your price. If you feel strongly that lowering the price to help people out must be done, do it. Helping people is something you should be proud of. Just don't do it to a point where it hurts you or them.

Make sure you're still serving your ideal learner. Don't price yourself right out of your target market. Yes, it is possible to price yourself *below* your market. Some markets see lower price tags as a potential sign of low value. Know your market. Help people but don't sacrifice your entire business just because of a temporary event.

The big takeaway here is to avoid impulsively lowering prices when you get a moment of concern over the market. Frequent price changes erode buyer confidence in your offer.

Okay! Wasn't that discussion about inflation, impulse changes, and experimentation just the best? I know this is the stuff of nightmares for many business owners. Let's discuss something a little less soul-crushing: sales volume!

CHAPTER EIGHT

THE RELATIONSHIP BETWEEN VOLUME AND PRICE

Whenever you sell anything, you're selling it for a certain price. You want to sell a number of those products, and the quantity is the volume.

Wouldn't it be awesome if you sold a bunch of high-priced items? Hecks yeah, it would!

Normally, lower-priced items sell in higher volume. The inverse is also common. You may sell less of a higher-priced item because fewer people have access to that higher amount of money. This is the most basic way to view the relationship between volume and price.

Now, what constitutes a low or high price? All the things discussed in Chapter Two! We're not talking luxury cars or entry-level sedan prices here, folks. Everything is relative to the market you play in.

Let's look at an example to make this clear. Suppose I have a target of $100,000 in revenue through sales. If I'm strictly selling $20 books, I have to sell five thousand books to hit my $100,000 revenue target. Next, we sell a coaching program for $5,000. I need to sell twenty coaching programs at $5,000 each to hit the target of $100,000. That's a big difference in volume! Of course, there's a big price difference as well, but the volume really changes how you capture those sales.

There is a completely different energy and plan associated with selling the books versus the coaching programs in the example. Some people see the expense of one as more challenging than the other based on whether they like selling and marketing bulk items.

If you're the type of person who enjoys marketing and sales, then the prospect of selling many things may not seem like a big deal to you, right? People not experienced with marketing and sales may find selling two thousand or five thousand items difficult; having a higher-ticket item at a lower-volume target might be better.

Now, let's say you have something in the middle. You have a $2,000 course, for example. It's not the $5,000 high-ticket item, and it's not the $20 lower-ticket item. It's priced in the middle at $2,000, and you must sell fifty of those to hit your target. That's a good compromise. When applied to an individual product, you can see where the relationship between the price and volume really matters.

Now if you heard me mention courses, coaching programs, and books, and you're automatically thinking, *I wrote the book; right now, I just need to market my product and sell it. That's different from providing one-on-one coaching.* Well, you're absolutely correct.

You can spend equal amounts of time and energy on marketing and sales on any of those products or services to reach your revenue goals. Just because a particular product has a lower price doesn't mean it's easier to sell. And just because another has a higher price doesn't mean it's harder to sell.

Each of these individual products and services has its own unique relationship with sales value.

There is a significant difference in the energy a person will spend on providing a service versus developing and selling a product.

Okay, so what do I mean by that?

Services are more demanding of the provider's energy than products. There may be a tremendous amount of energy invested up front to develop a product. But once it exists, it's ready to market and sell. The product stands very much on its own to a certain degree. At that point, you spend less energy to maintain the value and ensure client satisfaction.

If you buy a book, the enjoyment of reading is what you expect to make you happy. You expect the author to write and publish a solid book. You don't expect the author to show up at your house every time you read that book (although that could be pretty cool!). You don't schedule a meeting for them to read the book to you or answer your questions while you're reading it, right? Therein lies the difference.

Let's consider an example of a coaching program that includes coursework. A coaching program may include predeveloped products, such as worksheets, course lessons, and a journal. The coach and client will interact in regularly scheduled sessions. *They spend time (which is money) together.*

That increases the price. So, coaching and consulting programs are normally high-priced, low-volume offers. It makes sense, right?

What happens if you price the same program too low? You'll spend the same time and energy on the effort for less money. That's what happens. You'll need more clients to make a decent living. Worst case, you don't attract enough clients (low volume), and the few clients you have can't keep your business afloat because of your low prices.

PERCEIVED VALUE

Want some unavoidable truth? In markets that lack pricing norms, people associate value with price. As I stated earlier, most online course markets are too young to experience these norms. That means your price reflects your perceived value.

Let's revisit our coaching program example. If you charge the low price of $150 for your coaching program, people may think there's little value for them. After all, they know coaches who charge much more for their programs. What makes your offer less valuable?

Most coaches charge more than that per hour! They're not even looking at your program for $150 because they feel there's nothing there for them.

It is not the consumer's responsibility to know whether you priced your program appropriately. Your offer must accurately express its value. Usually, when the price is higher, people perceive higher value. And they expect better quality because of the price. They see quality as part of that value.

Quality consulting and coaching programs often use the higher-priced, lower-volume model.

You find this with consulting rates, coaching programs, and masterminds. Face-to-face investments at higher rates.

ONLINE COURSES

Online courses often fall somewhere in the middle of the spectrum for digital products because they are very flexible. They involve making an up-front investment in course materials, recording lessons, and building the site. But they don't require as much one-on-one time with clients. *But they aren't low in value because well-built courses lead to a valuable outcome for the learner.*

You invested time and energy into your course, making it valuable to the learner, and thus it should be priced appropriately.

Whether you sell a course for $500 or $3,000, it must be appropriate for your client and the type of course that you deliver. Because you are a professional, you use an LMS, like Thinkific, and create something people actually need. If you are solving your learner's problem and helping them make money with the outcomes from your course, you can demand a higher price.

In that case, you'd most likely expect a lower volume of sales at a higher price point. In a fantastic scenario, your higher-price course comes with a high sales volume, and the world is just peachy. You'd be super stoked if that happened, right?

But normally, higher-priced programs have a lower sales volume. *They also experience a lower volume of refunds and dissatisfaction.* So do with that what you will.

Lower-priced course options include minicourses or micro-learning courses. These courses can be very valuable and matter significantly to the learner, but they are shorter in content, deliver less impact, and have less application focus (fewer worksheets, exercises, etc.). They also require less time commitment. You can expect a higher sales volume on these courses if the market is big, competition is moderate to low, and people dig your brand.

Suppose you have a high-dollar flagship course to which you've dedicated a significant amount of quality, time, and money. It absolutely solves problems, informs learners, and helps them close a performance gap. That's worth money to them. If you price the course at or below that value, then great, you're doing good, and you should expect to make good money on that.

So, what's my advice? I recommend that you consider your specific situation and do what works best for you and your clients—investing in relationships and collaboration. Look into the higher-priced, lower-volume model.

I'll give you an example.

Outside of my passive product sales (books and on-demand courses), I provide a select number of clients with premium, value-driven services. I want those clients to never think twice about my price because they get a big return on investment with me. I apply this thinking to virtual or in-person courses, workshops, masterminds, and coaching programs.

The recipient's return on investment is larger than the revenue earned through selling their products after working with me. It includes the relationship we develop and the confidence they gain from the program. All of that is worth money to me and the people I work with.

I'm very sensitive to building a great relationship from the start (think: investment). If I am not a good fit for an individual, I encourage them to work with someone else. I don't force a round peg into a square hole. They are a good fit for my offer, or they are not. Keep it simple; don't get desperate for a sale and start bending like a gymnast to make price concessions for everyone who drops into your inbox.

There you go. My clients and I are both happy; that's the priority.

That's an example of intentionally building a product line that does not require high-volume sales to survive. I invert the price and volume plans for my passive products.

Should you also sell products? I am so happy you asked.

The short answer is yes. I love to develop products. I'm a content creator who enjoys the creative process. The big change in this situation is applying my marketing and sales energy in a different way.

I don't do one or the other; I enjoy both models! When both make you happy, like they do in my situation, you need to be very careful to balance the two.

I can take on as many clients as come in the door. I'm happy to serve with my time and energy, but I reserve enough of both to write new books and articles, develop new courses, record podcasts, and market all of it.

You definitely need to experience doing both to determine where your balance lies. I messed this up once (or twice) and took on more one-on-one clients than I normally do. The money was too good to turn down, or so I thought. My product development quickly ground to a halt as I invested myself in my clients. My excitement for the day went bye-bye faster than I expected. I became tired and out of balance. I would have been happier with more balance.

Every morning, when you wake up, I want you to think about serving your business, your clients, your family, and yourself.

What would make you happy and still get your bills paid?

Do you want an empire of products, services, and employees? This comes with a significant administrative workload. Think: big revenue with big expenses.

Would low-priced, high-volume sales be the best thing since sliced bread? This requires a strong marketing effort. Think: cast a big net to catch lots of fish (buyers).

Or would you rather have higher-priced items with low-volume sales? This requires lots of relationship building, networking, unmistakable expertise in your field, and trust.

Think: investing in more intimate marketing and longer sales cycles.

Or...would you like to mix them a bit like I do? Think: high energy output focusing constantly on maintaining balance.

There are different risks, emotions, and investments involved in each option. Take some time to think things through, reflect on the business you want (not just the business you can have), and do what's right for *you*.

Anything is possible if the fit is right!

All the experts who tell you how to do things should instead tell you what's possible. It's up to you to figure out what's best for your business.

I'm sharing what I've seen work, not insisting that no other options exist. I will never tell you that there are only one or two ways to do things. Make the business you want, not necessarily the one you can have.

> **JUST BECAUSE YOU *CAN* DO SOMETHING DOESN'T MEAN YOU *SHOULD*.**

Think about your business plan for next year. Did you develop the right products and offers with a pricing and volume strategy that serves you and your clients in the best way possible? If the answer is no, then think about how to get where you need to be.

Storytime! When I founded EAST Partnership, I created unique and valuable courses for maintenance and reliability engineers. The courses help these niche engineers do better work.

Value? Check!

Right audience? Check!

Sales? Not so much...

How could that be? Was it my price?

I had a decent mid-market price point. Not too low, and definitely not too high. The price didn't give the impression of inferior quality. I didn't have much competition, so I had to be careful. And people responded well to the course. I never had a request for a refund. It was a good quality product, and people were happy. I spent time with people who attended my courses and everyone was doing well.

But I couldn't figure out why we weren't selling more. I knew this product would help many people.

Then I discovered I had made two fatal errors.

Initially, I marketed to the engineers, but after about a year, I realized I was selling to the wrong person. I built the course for the engineer, as I should. But the valuable outcome wasn't theirs...it was their boss's!

I should have been selling it to the engineer's boss. I was asking the engineer to spend their personal money on fixing their boss's problem. That was a fatal error in my pricing strategy.

I built a medium-priced course and had a low volume of sales when I was expecting a medium volume of sales at a medium price. I had realistic expectations, but I'd targeted the wrong person. Once I shifted to a business-to-business (B2B) marketing approach and sold to organizations, we had four times the sales.

Yep...four times the sales! This is where I firmly planted my palm on my forehead.

Rather than take action before we identified the problem, we focused on finding the root cause of our poor sales. We didn't panic and change the price, invest time and money in new tech, or dump funds in advertising. We found the right problem to solve, then attacked it with vigor.

Our new sales volume matched the volume and pricing strategy that we initially set for our courses. Sweet!

So, what was the second mistake? Well, before I identified the real issue, I did what a lot of people did: I panicked and ran a sales promotion any time I could. Essentially, it gave me an excuse to offer my product at a lower price without lowering the real price.

Who was I fooling? Me. I clearly didn't respect the price of my course.

I realized that my knee-jerk reaction of running holiday sales caused people watching us closely on social media to stall! They expected us to run a sale in three months or *insert any event here, Taco Tuesday included.* They waited us out!

I scaled back my sales promotions and discounted prices. I did that and simultaneously increased our exposure to B2B marketing. Ultimately, we improved sales and revenue. We were now serving our *business* better.

I was hyper-focused on providing an appropriate price for the learners. I reached out to every student and asked them how they felt about the value and experience of the course. Fortunately, everyone I talked to said the course price was great—not too low, not too high.

When your courses aren't selling, remember that price is a simple thing that easily gets blamed for problems it doesn't cause. Make sure the price is the problem before you change it.

There are many reasons a course may not sell. Slight changes to your overall strategy can have a big impact, especially when marketing is consistent. My company would immediately see an increase in sales when we were talking about our projects and products with the right people. It's funny how that works (dripping sarcasm).

My mentor, Honorée Corder, will tell you, "A book in motion is money in motion, and a book at rest is money at rest." You could say the same thing about courses.

> A COURSE IN MOTION IS MONEY IN MOTION, AND A COURSE AT REST IS MONEY AT REST.

The moral of the story? Have realistic expectations about sales volume and price. Don't panic and drop the price when things aren't working as you expect. Find out what's really going on. Start with consistent marketing to the right audience, in the right ways, in the right places. If the price is the problem, you'll hear about it.

CHAPTER NINE

TAXES FOR ONLINE COURSES AND THE IMPACT ON PRICING

Our next topic is about the wonderful world of sales taxes. Most people cringe a little at this topic. That's cool; we might be related.

You may not have that reaction if you are the type who gets a kick out of writing a check to the government when your taxes are due. Well, this next part will probably still make you cringe because sales taxes are especially difficult to navigate in online course sales.

A quick disclaimer: I'm most definitely ___not___ an accountant or tax professional, so this is not accounting or tax advice. I recommend you seek professional guidance, just like I did, to keep your taxes legit. I'm not that guy.

Okay, back to the not-legally-binding advice!

Some counties, states, and countries require sales tax on digital courses. Others do not. And sales tax rules apply at the location of the purchaser, not the seller.

Yep, you read that correctly. You are responsible for abiding by the sales tax laws of *your buyer's location*. That makes selling digital products to buyers around the world very...exciting.

The simplest example of how this *should* work? Here you go: Local, state, and federal governments set sales tax laws. We collect and pay those taxes on behalf of our business. Because of this, we set a price for our course, then charge tax in addition to that price. Then, we report the amount earned and issue payment to the appropriate governing body.

If only it were this simple.

There is no single standard sales tax for online courses. There isn't even a standard government definition of what makes up an online course!

So, you have many government entities, each defining sales taxes for online courses differently. Some define it so loosely that we can interpret it in several ways. This is both a strength and a weakness.

We also have the problem that, in many states, sales taxes are based on the location of *the buyer, not the seller.* This is referred to as a destination-based sales tax approach. Other governments (state governments in the US) determine sales tax rates by the location of the vendor. We refer to this as origin-based sales taxing.

In my opinion, this is the single biggest problem with taxing online courses or any online digital product. We must track taxes according to so many different laws. And if you're selling internationally, that can get very confusing very quickly.

You're probably thinking, *Oh my gosh, what am I getting myself into?* Just breathe.

There are literally thousands of online course creators out there doing the same thing you're planning to do. And they all seem to survive somehow, some way.

CHARGING ONE FEE, WHICH INCLUDES THE TAX

Many of us rely on sales processors like PayPal, Stripe, or Thinkific Payments to collect money from customers at checkout. Some systems collect purchase location data for you but don't charge tax. The person buying the course sees the price you set for the course without an additional tax.

These systems track the location of your sale by ZIP code or by the reported location from the credit card address of the buyer through the payment processor. The system collects that data and tells you, the seller, whether you will owe sales tax for a purchase in that location. Then it's up to you to remit the tax from that sale to the government.

Some course sellers find software like Quaderno helpful. At the time of this writing, Quaderno calculates the sales tax for every purchase and tells the seller who to remit to. This is a step beyond what most of the payment processors are currently capable of doing.

In the scenarios I've just described, you charge one price. That price includes the purchase price + estimated tax. You deduct taxes after the sale and remit them to the government.

CHARGING A PURCHASE PRICE AND TAX SEPARATELY

Companies attempt to resolve this problem, including Stripe and Thinkific Payments. In fact, it's one of the embedded functions of the Thinkific LMS. These companies realize how important sales tax collection and remittance are for course sellers. And if they can harness this and ease our burden, they will win us over.

At the time of this writing, Thinkific Payments is beta testing a total online tax collection and remittance program in North America. This will be a game changer if they pull it off! They will charge, collect, and remit the tax for you.

Who knows, by the time this book ends up in your hands, they may have cracked the case, and we can address taxes more easily.

THE TAX LANDSCAPE

One thing that won't change, though, is the complexity of the tax landscape. And that is that the state and local governments may set their own sales tax.

Let's briefly address this, and I mean *briefly*, because I don't want to talk about taxes any more than you want to read about them.

Federal governments set a base tax, while states or provinces add additional taxes. Finally, local governments add the last layer. I know, it's the least tasty sandwich ever.

Sales tax in the US and Canada is primarily controlled by states and provinces. These governments can define sales tax laws and determine sales tax for the exchanges of goods within their borders here in the US.

There are fifty states potentially managing fifty different approaches to sales tax. This complexity is inherent in our governmental model, and there's no way around it.

However, your courses *may* fit into a nontaxable definition if you classify them as a service. Let me explain.

Tangible property (a product) is normally taxable. But services are tax exempt in many locations. Some locales will impose a service tax if you perform services over a certain dollar amount in that area.

For example, in some states, you owe them a tax if you do $100,000 worth of sales and services within their border. They set a limit and collect taxes from businesses making large profits in the state.

I don't know about you, but I love doing more than $100,000 worth of consumer business in any state, so I welcome this problem. I'll gladly pay those taxes. The point here is that you need to be aware of how this shakes out for your business.

One way that they may consider your course a service rather than a product is if it's live or has a significant number of live components to it. When you deliver physical products to your learners, you're dwelling in the land of tangible product sales.

I'm not advocating that you create a hybrid course where you teach part of it live online, and then throw your hands in the air and say, *Oh, that's it; I'm done. I don't have to pay sales tax for all services and no products.* It's your accountant's job to help you determine whether your offer qualifies as a nontaxable service.

That is the biggest lesson to take away from this chapter. You need help with taxes. You may manage a few sales for a short period and fly under the radar for a while. But eventually, if you're running a serious business, you could get into a bind. Properly manage your business taxes with a professional. Dot your i's and cross your t's.

One last point on taxes: It doesn't matter who you hire to help you or what software you purchase to track, manage, and calculate your taxes. It also doesn't matter who buys your courses, what payment processing system you use, or what collection method you use.

> ### IN THE END, THE ONLY PERSON RESPONSIBLE FOR PAYING THE TAX IS *YOU.*

Sales taxes are *your* responsibility, and only *you* will pay for mismanaging them. Not to sound ominous, but it's on you to get this right, and if you don't, there will be financial implications when the taxman comes calling.

You may think that sales tax isn't that big a deal. Where I live, it's about 5 percent. That can end up being a lot of money over time. The last thing we want to do is realize we owe back taxes for ten years and not have that money set aside to pay.

Most people don't have ten years of 5 percent of their money set aside to spend on taxes, just in case. They have set aside money for retirement or a major investment but not "what if" tax funds.

I encourage you to get your arms around this with your accountant, set the money aside as soon as you collect a payment, and pay your taxes on time. It's part of business ownership. It's true that it's complex, but we must exist in this system. So do what's right to make it work.

Okay, enough of that tax stuff. Let's wrap this party up and get your courses out there!

CHAPTER TEN

FINAL TAKEAWAYS FOR SUCCESS

You did it! Congratulations on gaining the knowledge and confidence to create a course pricing strategy that serves your clients and your business. As I stated in the beginning, the topic of pricing is subjective and personal. However, you now know how to consider the four points for building your course strategy. To recap, those four points are

1. Competitor prices

2. The value of the outcome for the learner

3. The cost of course delivery

4. Industry norms and buyer habits

Looking at these points, you can now recognize the influence of the market and business environment on your prices. Do you see common static like personal motivations, insecurities, or bad habits included in that list? No way! Those things often drive course creators to insufficiently price their courses. I've pointed you toward observable conditions and traceable measurements. Although pricing is subjective, it can be managed professionally and with confidence in your market observations.

You also learned about the many payment options including single payments, payment plans, subscriptions, site membership, and combinations of these options! You can now consider which of these approaches best suits your customers and offers.

We then discussed why you should avoid pricing your courses strictly by time and materials. You now know when it is appropriate to use this approach and why doing so can be detrimental in the wrong situations.

One of the most important discussions involved the force multipliers of affiliate and revenue share partners. Allow me to say it one more time—you should *definitely* consider leveraging these relationships to grow your business. You now understand how affiliate and revenue share partners impact your prices and how to incorporate them into your sales system.

Speaking of sales, have you reassessed your relationship with sales promotions? Are you committed to a planned promotion schedule and limiting the frequency of sales promotions to truly unique and beneficial events? Good! I'm sure you've also identified the reasons to raise or lower your prices based on performance and business drivers.

Those two chapters are very important for managing prices for the life of your courses.

Of course, you have to launch your courses before you can maintain them. You are now prepared to choose a beneficial launch strategy regardless of whether you decide to presell or beta test your course or not.

We went even deeper when we explored the relationship between volume and price and the perceived value of your offer. These concepts are critical to building a healthy expectation for the number of course sales needed to support your business at chosen prices. Sell cheaper courses, and your dependency on larger sales numbers naturally climbs. Sell higher-priced courses, and you may survive on fewer sales. You also know which approach is best for your ideal buyer because of how prices impact perceived value.

It's almost hard to believe the party ended with the most exciting topic—taxes. Yeah, we took no prisoners! I do not doubt that you'll determine exactly what you should pay in taxes, how you'll charge for them, and when you'll remit them to the appropriate governing bodies. Then, you'll tell all your friends about how adult you are after paying those taxes and drop a good Dad Joke or two to drive the point home.

When you get a chance, let me know how things go for you. I mean it! I want to hear all about your challenges and successes. Send me an email or contact me on social media to tell me how things go after you put this book to work for your business.

Okay, now get out there and make the world a better place with your courses!

QUICK FAVOR

Thank you so much for dedicating your time to reading this book! May I ask a quick favor?

Will you please take a moment to leave a review on Amazon, Goodreads, or wherever you purchased the book? Your words have power. Your review can help this book serve more people. I appreciate you!

GRATITUDE

My thanks start with Tammie, my wife and confidant. Thank you for enduring my pacing and ranting every time I had an idea for the book. You are an expert at making my dreams possible. Without your support, being an author and entrepreneur would be impossible.

Caleb—thank you for the internet, server farm, video edits, and road trip to Nashville! Watching you grow into a young entrepreneur is such a wonderful experience for me. I love you, dude.

Gabriel—your footsteps above my head set the beat to the soundtrack of this book. Every word was written to the sound of you having an absolute blast in the room above me. Love you!

Maddie—your eyes light up every time I talk about a book with you. Your love for reading, art, and life fill me with youthful energy. You are truly my kid. I love you, little!

The all-star team of writing and publishing excellence takes home another win! Honorée Corder (mentorship), Karen Hunsanger (edits), Dino Marino (design),

Catherine Turner (proofreading), and Brian Meeks (book description)—you rock! You took this book to another level!

Karen—thank you for being flexible, responsive, organized, and so darn good at your job! We've made yet another book idea a reality. Thank you for your enduring awesomeness! THANK YOU!

Honorée—what can I say? You are the best mentor and friend an author could have! I continue to be blessed with your friendship and guidance. Most importantly, you believe in what I'm doing. Thank you for setting the pace and the vision!

Get a comprehensive education in online course creation, marketing, and business with these courses and programs at www.marinotraining.com

Build Your Online Course
with Lucas Marino

◢◢ MARINO

Learn
THINKIFIC

◢◢ MARINO

If you are looking for an online community of creative entrepreneurs, consider the Empire Builders Masterclass. We offer something for every creative entrepreneur, including an online community, blogs, videos, and courses to help you build your books, courses, mindset, business, and more!

Learn more at
www.empirebuildersmasterclass.com

WHO IS LUCAS MARINO?

Dr. Lucas C. Marino, PMP, is the founder and owner of Marino Consulting Services, LLC, and his two training companies, Marino Training and EAST Partnership. He is also cofounder of the Empire Builder's Masterclass, a training resource for creative entrepreneurs.

Lucas helps entrepreneurs and authors launch and sustain online training products. He is a Certified Thinkific Expert, author of *Monetize Your Book with a Course,* and host of the *Conversations with Course Creators* podcast.

A military engineer by experience, he spent twenty-one years as a naval engineer in the United States Coast Guard. He then founded Marino Consulting Services, LLC, and worked in several senior logistics engineering program manager roles for military acquisitions, including Army landing craft and the Navy's COLUMBIA submarine program. Then he decided the time was right to realize his dream of being a creative entrepreneur, and he made the big leap!

He received his MS in Systems Engineering and Doctor of Engineering degrees from the George Washington University.

Lucas has a passion for developing others and partnering with entrepreneurs!

Marino Training
Email: lucas@marinotraining.com
Marino Training: www.marinotraining.com

Empire Builders Masterclass:
https://www.empirebuildersmasterclass.com/

LinkedIn:
https://www.linkedin.com/in/lucas-marino-deng/

LinkedIn Company Page:
https://www.linkedin.com/company/marino-training/

Twitter:
https://twitter.com/marino_training

Facebook Page:
https://www.facebook.com/marinotraining

Facebook Private Group:
https://www.facebook.com/groups
/monetizeyourbookwithacourse/